Community
Leaders

Then and Now

Christina Hill, M.A.
and Torrey Maloof

Property of

Associate Editor
Christina Hill, M.A.

Assistant Editor
Torrey Maloof

Editorial Director
Emily R. Smith, M.A.Ed.

Editor-in-Chief
Sharon Coan, M.S.Ed.

Editorial Manager
Gisela Lee, M.A.

Creative Director
Lee Aucoin

Illustration Manager
Timothy J. Bradley

Designer
Lesley Palmer
Debora Brown
Zac Calbert
Robin Erickson

Project Consultant
Corinne Burton, M.A.Ed.

Publisher
Rachelle Cracchiolo, M.S.Ed.

Teacher Created Materials
5301 Oceanus Drive
Huntington Beach, CA 92649-1030
http://www.tcmpub.com
ISBN 978-0-7439-9385-2
© 2007 by Teacher Created Materials, Inc.
Reprinted 2012

Table of Contents

What Is a Community Leader?

There are many kinds of **communities** (kuh-MEW-nuh-teez). A community can be the place where you live. Or, it can be a group of people who like the same things. A community is a group of people who work together as a team.

⬇ Senator Barack Obama speaks at a town hall meeting.

4

Communities have leaders. These leaders do many kinds of jobs. But, they all have the same goal. They help to make their communities better. These leaders make plans. And, they help people who are in need.

A Sizable Difference

Communities can be very big. Or, they can be very small. New York City is a community. It has over 8 million (MIL-yuhn) people! A small town called Victory in the state of Vermont is also a community. They have fewer than 100 people.

Parent Teacher Association

Do you know what the PTA is? The letters *PTA* stand for Parent Teacher Association (uh-so-see-AY-shuhn). The PTA helps parents work with their children's schools.

Every PTA has a **president** (PREZ-uh-duhnt). This person is a **volunteer** (VOL-uhn-teer) from the community. He or she helps run the PTA. The PTA president meets with parents and teachers. They talk about school. The school may have problems. The PTA president works hard to help solve these problems.

A PTA meeting in 1960 ➡

Getting Started

Phoebe Hearst (FEE-bee HUHRST) started the first PTA. She called it the National (NASH-uh-nuhl) Congress of Mothers. She was a teacher. And, she was a mother. She wanted mothers and teachers to work together. This group became the PTA. Today, it is not just for mothers. Any parent or teacher can join.

Phoebe Hearst

The PTA raised money for students ➡ to go on this field trip to the zoo.

▲ This principal welcomes a new student.

School Principal

Did you know that your school **principal** (PRIN-suh-puhl) is a community leader? Principals help run schools. They help teachers solve problems. They keep order in their schools. They help keep students and teachers safe.

Principals make sure students learn the skills they need. They meet with parents and teachers. Principals work hard to make sure their students do well on tests. They want what is best for their schools.

One-Room Schools

Schools used to be just one classroom. There was only one teacher. The teacher would teach all grade levels at the same time! There were no school principals. But, schools began to grow. They needed principals to help run the schools.

▲ One-room school

▼ This principal runs her school's spelling bee.

You Are Not in Trouble

Some students think that principals are only there to **discipline** (DIS-uh-plihn) them. That is far from true. They are there to help their students. Some principals used to work as teachers. They still work to make sure that students learn.

Youth Leaders

Are you a Girl Scout or Boy Scout? Or, do you go to the Boys and Girls Club after school? If so, then you know how great youth leaders can be. Youth leaders are community leaders. They work hard to help young boys and girls.

These leaders plan meetings and camping trips. They play games with their groups. They teach children skills. Youth leaders teach children to be a part of a team.

⬥ A Boy Scout and a Girl Scout salute the flag in 1960.

Crazy for Cookies

Girl Scouts sell cookies. Nearly 200 million boxes of cookies are sold every year! The money made goes to the Girl Scouts. The money helps pay for future Girl Scout events.

▲ Former Los Angeles mayor James Hahn and his son buy Girl Scout cookies.

Neil ➡ Armstrong

A Boy Scout on the Moon?

Some Boy Scouts have gone on to become United States presidents! A lot of famous people were once Boy Scouts. Neil Armstrong was an Eagle Scout. That is the highest level of Boy Scout. The Boy Scouts gave Armstrong many awards. They were proud that a Boy Scout was the first man to walk on the moon!

11

Charity Leaders

A **charity** (CHAIR-uh-tee) is a group that helps others. Some groups collect money or food and clothes. These things help people in need. Some groups help sick people. Others just help children. They may collect gifts. Then, they give these gifts to children on holidays.

Charity leaders plan events. These events make money. A leader can plan to have a bake sale. Then, the money from the bake sale can go to a good cause. Some groups have food drives. The food goes to people who do not have enough to eat. Charity leaders give their time to help others.

⬇ These volunteers sort food at a food drive.

You Can Donate, Too!

Students can help raise money, too. A great way is to have a car wash. All it takes is a bucket, a hose, and some soap. Plus, you will need lots of students ready for hard work!

The Salvation Army

William Booth and his wife wanted to start a charity. Their group became The Salvation (sal-VAY-shuhn) Army. This charity group assists people who are in need all over the world. They give food and clothing. And, they find homes for people who do not have places to live.

William Booth

↑ This business leader is helping her community.

Business Leaders

Did you know that big companies (KUHM-puh-neez) have leaders, too? These leaders help the **business** (BIZ-nuhs) world. And, they also help their communities. Some business leaders give money to their communities. Others give their time.

Business leaders can share their skills. They can speak to students. Some teach college classes. They teach people how to start new companies. Business leaders also offer new jobs. New jobs help many people in the community.

30 Billion Dollars!

Warren Buffet is the head of a big company. He is a business leader. His company makes a lot of money. But, Buffet thinks it is wrong to keep all that money. So, he gives money to charity. Once, he gave 30 billion dollars to one charity! No one had ever given that much money to a charity before.

↟ Warren Buffet and his wife

↡ Business meeting

Government Leaders

Do you know who solves problems and makes laws for our community? This is the job of the **government** (GUHV-uhrn-muhnt). Each community has many government leaders. We vote for them. They help make big **decisions** (dih-SIZH-uhnz) for our community.

Women line up ➡ to vote long ago.

Let's Vote on It

Any **citizen** (SIT-uh-zuhn) who is at least 18 years old can vote in the United States. But, it was not always that way. Long ago, only certain men had the right to vote. Women did not like this. They wanted to vote, too. In 1920, women got the right to vote.

Judges (JUHJ-ehz) are community leaders. They work in courts of law. They decide what each law means. **Mayors** (MAY-uhrz) are in charge of cities. They make sure the people in their cities are safe. City or town **councils** (KOWN-sills) make the rules for cities and towns. Men and women from the community are elected to be on a council. Most neighborhoods (NAY-ber-hoodz) also have leaders. They make sure people in the neighborhood follow the rules.

Everybody is Welcome

Do you know that citizens can attend council meetings? They can speak to the council about any concerns. This helps the mayor make the right choices for the city. Some meetings are shown on television. And, some can even be watched on the Internet!

↟ This cardinal is speaking on Easter Sunday.

◂ Young Buddhist monks

Religious Leaders

There are a lot of **religions** (rih-LIJ-uhnz) in the world. Religion helps people make sense of their lives. Religious leaders help their communities. They help people understand the world. They listen to people's problems. They also give advice.

↓ The Qur'an is a sacred book of Islam.

↑ This rabbi reads to a young boy.

Special Books

Each religion has a book. These books tell the history of the religion. Religious leaders know these books very well. They use these books to guide others.

Each religion has leaders. Christians (KRIS-chuhnz) have leaders called pastors or priests. The Jewish religion has rabbis (RAH-biyz). There are many other kinds of religious leaders. All of these leaders share the same goal. They want to help others.

Community Cleanup

Many community leaders work to keep their communities clean. They pick up trash on beaches. They help clean up neighborhood parks. Some people help plant new trees. They work hard to keep their communities healthy. These people are good role models.

Storms can cause a lot of damage (DAM-ihj). Too much rain can cause flooding. Homes are ruined. Many people help clean up after a storm. They fix and rebuild homes. They help put the damaged community back together.

Red Cross ➡ workers help a man who is hurt.

◀ This woman helps clean up her local beach.

Habitat for Humanity

Habitat for Humanity (HAB-uh-tat for hyuh-MAN-uh-tee) helps build houses. The houses are for people who do not have homes. The houses are sold at low prices. Many people come to help out. The group has built over 200,000 houses. In 2005, a bad storm hit the United States. It was called Hurricane Katrina (HUHR-uh-kane KUH-tree-nuh). Many people lost their homes. Habitat for Humanity helped rebuild homes.

Former President ➡ Jimmy Carter helps to build a home.

Red Cross

The American Red Cross helps out in disasters (dih-ZAHS-tuhrz). They hold blood drives so people can give blood. They even have classes. These classes teach people how to be safe.

A Great Place to Live

Community leaders help make a community a great place to live. What would your school be like without your principal's help? What would our country be like without government leaders? Our communities would fall apart. These leaders help to keep community members happy and safe. They also make sure that we all work together as a team.

Community leaders give their time to help others. They are caring and kind. Many people look to them as role models. They **inspire** (in-SPYER) members of a community to do their best. Do you know any leaders in your community?

▲ This youth group leader is teaching children about nature.

A Day in the Life Then

Juliette Gordon Low (1860–1927)

Juliette (joo-LEE-uht) Gordon Low wanted to help her community. But, she did not know how. One day, she met the leader of the Boy Scouts. He told her about the program. She thought it was a great idea. But, there was not a group for girls! She thought this group would be great for the girls in her community. So, she started the Girl Scouts.

Let's pretend to ask Juliette Gordon Low some questions about her job.

Why do you think the Girl Scouts are important?

Girls are always taught how to do things indoors. They know how to cook and clean.

But, there are important skills that can be learned outdoors. Girl Scouts learn how to take care of themselves. They learn to be confident.

What is your day like?

We meet as a group. The girls learn something new every week. This week, the girls are learning how to swim.

What do you like most about your job?

I like being a community leader. I have started a group that will last a long time. There will always be girls who want to learn new things. And, the Girl Scouts will be there to teach them.

This group of Girl → Scouts met First Ladies Mrs. Coolidge and Mrs. Hoover.

Tools of the Trade Then

These women were Red Cross nurses. They took supplies on a train. These supplies were given to soldiers. The trains were helpful tools for the Red Cross.

This is a poster from World War II. The United States needed money for the war. The poster asked children to buy war stamps. The money from the stamps was used to help the soldiers.

The Nineteenth Amendment gave women the right to vote. This was a very important tool for communities. It let women help choose their leaders.

Tools of the Trade Now

- Soldiers still go to war. And, they still need supplies. Red Cross workers today can send supplies by airplane. This is an easier way to help. And, it is much faster!

- Voting is a very important tool. Most community leaders wear pins and stickers on voting day. This is to remind other people in their communities to vote.

▲ These boys are selling lemonade. The mayor of their town will collect the money. The money will be used to build a new park in their town. These boys are helping to make their community a better place.

A Day in the Life Now

Kim Hood

Kim Hood is a Girl Scout troop leader. She lives in Illinois (ill-uh-NOI). She works hard to help the girls in her community. She is very active! Mrs. Hood loves roller skating. She even owns her own roller-skating rink! She loves to rock climb. And, she loves to camp, make crafts, and play games with her family.

When did you decide to become a Girl Scout troop leader?

I have three daughters. My oldest daughter wanted to join Girl Scouts. That was when she was in kindergarten. It seemed like a great adventure! So, I became a troop leader. Now, I have been a troop leader for 14 years!

What is your day as a troop leader like?

I work with older girls now. We do a lot of activities. And, we do a lot of things to help our community. We have fundraisers. Then, we have meetings where the girls can earn badges. My day is busy! I help plan the activities. I also have to get things ready for the meetings. And, I set goals for the girls. We work together as a team. We break things down into steps. This is how we reach our goals. It is fun to work as a team to make things happen.

▲ This is Kim Hood with her daughter, Sydney.

What do you like most about your job?

I love to watch the girls try new things. I like being a part of a youth group. Our group builds confidence and community awareness. And, I like to eat s'mores and sing silly songs around a campfire. You only get to be young for so long!

Glossary

business—the making, buying, and selling of goods and services

charity—giving aid to the poor or needy

citizen—a member of a city or town

communities—people living in a place together

councils—leading groups in cities and towns

decisions—making choices

discipline—system of rules; to control behavior

government—a political group that leads a city, state, or nation

inspire—to encourage, guide, or influence

judges—people who decide the outcome of a court case

mayors—the elected leaders of cities

president—the leader of a group, company, or country

principal—the leader of a school

religions—systems of beliefs and practices

volunteer—a person who helps others for free

Index

Credits

Acknowledgements

Special thanks to Kim Hood for providing the *Day in the Life Now* interview. Mrs. Hood is a Girl Scout troop leader in Illinois.

Image Credits

cover Greg Mathieson/Mai/Mai/Time Life Pictures/Getty Images; p.1 Greg Mathieson/Mai/Mai/Time Life Pictures/Getty Images; p.4 Tim Boyle/Getty Images; p.5 (top) Photos.com; p.5 (bottom) Geocris/Dreamstime.com; p.6 Ralph Crane/Time Life Pictures/Getty Images; p.7 (left) The Library of Congress; p.7 (right) Lisette Le Bon/SuperStock, Inc.; p.8 Christina Kennedy/Getty Images; p.9 (top) The Library of Congress; p.9 (bottom) Dirk Anschutz/Getty Images; p.10 H. Armstrong Roberts/Retrofile/Getty Images; p.11 (top) Justin Sullivan/Getty Images; p.11 (middle) Samantha Grandy/Shutterstock, Inc.; p.11 (bottom) NASA Kennedy Space Center; p.12 Kevin Moloney/Getty Images; p.13 (top) Robert W. Ginn/Alamy Images; p.13 (bottom) The Library of Congress; p.14 Igor Karon/Shutterstock, Inc.; p.15 (top) Brad Markel/Getty Images; p.15 (middle) Sebastian Kaulitzki/Shutterstock, Inc.; p.15 (bottom) Arrow Studio/Shutterstock, Inc.; p.16 The Library of Congress; p.17 Stephen Coburn/Shutterstock, Inc.; p.18 (left) Christine Gonsalves/Shutterstock, Inc.; p.18 (right) Mario Tama/Getty Images; p.19 (left) Taolmor/Shutterstock, Inc.; p.19 (right) The Library of Congress; p.20 Barbara Kennedy/Shutterstock, Inc.; pp.20–21 AFP/Getty Images; p.21 Erik S. Lesser/Getty Images; pp. 22–23 Bob Schatz/Getty Images; p.23 Jamie Wilson/Shutterstock, Inc.; p.24 Helen North/Hulton Archive/Getty Images; p.25 The Library of Congress; p.26 (top) The Library of Congress; p.26 (middle) The Library of Congress; p.26 (bottom) The National Archives; p.27 (top) Novastock/Alamy; p.27 (middle) Photos.com; p.27 (bottom) Donna Cuic/Shutterstock, Inc.; p.28 Courtesy of Kim Hood; p.29 Courtesy of Kim Hood; back cover The Library of Congress